Tom Wright is Research Professor of New Testament and Early Christianity at the University of St Andrews. He has written over seventy books, including the For Everyone guides to the New Testament, the highly acclaimed Christian Origins series and, most recently, *How God Became King*; *Creation, Power and Truth*, *Finding God in the Psalms*; and *Paul and the Faithfulness of God* (all published by SPCK).

Little Books of Guidance
Finding answers to life's big questions!

Also in the series:
How Do I Pray? by John Pritchard
What Do We Mean by 'God'? by Keith Ward
Where on Earth Is Heaven? by Paula Gooder

WHY READ THE BIBLE?

A little book of guidance

TOM WRIGHT

First published in Great Britain in 2015

Society for Promoting Christian Knowledge
36 Causton Street
London SW1P 4ST
www.spckpublishing.co.uk

British Library Cataloguing-in-Publication Data
A catalogue record for this book is available from the British Library

ISBN 978–0–281–07326–9
eBook ISBN 978–0–281–07327–6

Typeset by Graphicraft Limited, Hong Kong
First printed in China
Subsequently digitally printed in Great Britain

eBook by Graphicraft Limited, Hong Kong

Contents

Introduction

It's a big book, full of big stories with big characters. They have big ideas (not least about themselves) and make big mistakes. It's about God, and greed, and grace; about life, lust, laughter and loneliness. It's about birth, beginnings and betrayal; about siblings, squabbles and sex; about power and prayer and prison and passion.

And that's only Genesis.

The Bible itself, with Genesis as its majestic overture, is a huge, sprawling book. Imagine it as an enormous mural: if you painted all the figures life size, you'd need most of the Great Wall of China to display it. Picking it up, you need to remind yourself that you hold in your hands not only the most famous book in the world, but one which has extraordinary power to change lives, to change communities, to change the world.

But surely (someone will say) only God gets to change the world like that? How can we say that a mere *book* can do such a thing?

That's the strange thing. That's why the Bible is a vital, central element in Christian faith and life. Somehow, God seems to have delegated (as it were) some at least of the things he intends to do in the world to this book. It isn't quite like someone making a will, but nearly. It isn't quite like a composer writing a score for people to play, but it's not far off. It isn't exactly like a dramatist writing a play, but that gets quite close. It isn't even, though this is perhaps the sharpest so far, that the Bible is 'the story so far' in the true novel that God is still writing. It's all of these and more.

That, no doubt, is why there are so many fights about it. In fact, there are just as many battles *about* the Bible these days as there are battles within its pages.

1

What is the Bible?

So what is the Bible, and what should we be doing with it?

To begin with, the facts.

The Bible consists of two parts, which Christians refer to as the 'Old Testament' and the 'New Testament'. The Old Testament is much longer, nearly a thousand pages in the average printing, against the New Testament's three hundred. The Old Testament came into existence over a period of more than a millennium; the New, within less than a century.

The word 'Testament' is a translation of the word which also means 'covenant'. It is a central Christian claim that the events concerning Jesus were the means by which, in fulfilment of ancient Israelite prophecy, the creator God, Israel's God, renewed the covenant and thereby rescued the world. Many of the early Christian writings make the point by explicitly hooking on to the Old Testament, quoting or echoing it in order to offer themselves as the charter of that covenant renewal; hence, 'New Testament'. Calling the two parts by these related but differentiated names is thus a way of flagging up a claim and a question: the claim that the Jewish Bible remains a vital part of Christian scripture, and the question of how it is to be understood and applied by those who believe that its 'covenant' was indeed renewed in Jesus.

The books which Jews call the Bible, and Christians call the Old Testament, were grouped in three sections. The first five books (Genesis, Exodus, Leviticus, Numbers and Deuteronomy) were always regarded as special, and foundational. They are known as Torah ('Law'), and are traditionally ascribed to Moses himself. The next collection, known as the 'Prophets', include what we often think of as some of the historical books (1 and 2 Samuel, 1 and 2 Kings) as well as the books of the great prophets (Isaiah, Jeremiah, Ezekiel) and the so-called 'minor' prophets (Hosea and the rest). The third division, headed by the Psalms, is known simply as the 'Writings', and includes some very ancient material and some parts – such as the book of Daniel – which were only edited and accepted within the last 200 years BC. Even around the time of Jesus some were still debating whether all the 'Writings' (Esther and the Song of Solomon were particularly contentious) really belonged. Most thought they did, and so it has remained.

Torah, Prophets and Writings: 39 books in all. It may well be that the 'Law' and the 'Prophets' became fixed collections considerably earlier than the 'Writings'. One way or another, the three sections became the official list of the sacred books of the Jewish people. The Greek word for such an official list is 'canon', which means 'rule' or 'measuring rod'. That is the word that has been applied to them since the third or fourth century of the Christian era.

Most of these books are written in Hebrew, which is why the Old Testament is often referred to as 'the Hebrew Bible'. Parts of Daniel and Ezra, plus one verse in Jeremiah and two words in Genesis (a proper name), are in Aramaic, which is to classical Hebrew more or less what contemporary English is to Chaucer. Most scholars would agree that many if not all of the Old Testament books reached their final form through a process of editing. This may have been going on over many centuries, and may have involved considerable fresh writing. However, several books of which this is likely to be true (e.g. the prophet Isaiah) retain a remarkable inner coherence. Our knowledge of the original text of the Old Testament has been enormously enriched by the discovery of the Dead Sea Scrolls. They include copies of most of the Old Testament books, and show that the much later manuscripts upon which mainstream Judaism and Christianity have depended are very close, despite small variations, to the texts that would have been known in Jesus' day.

Over the 200 years or so before the time of Jesus, all these books were translated into Greek, probably in Egypt, for the benefit of the increasing number of Jews for whom Greek was the primary language. The Greek Bible they produced was, in various different versions, the one used by most early Christians. It is known as the 'Septuagint', because of stories about there having been 70 translators.

This is the point at which the books which came to be known as the 'Apocrypha' (literally, 'hidden things') first appear. A long and complex debate about their status and validity rumbled on in the early church, and re-emerged in the sixteenth and seventeenth centuries, as a result of which some Bibles include the Apocrypha and some do not. Those that do include them normally print the relevant books (sometimes adding some extra ones as well) in between the Old and the New Testaments, though the 'Jerusalem Bible' and other official Roman Catholic publications treat the Apocrypha simply as part of the Old Testament. Sadly, more people today are vaguely aware that these books have been controversial than have ever read them for themselves. At the very least, these books (like other works of the period, such as the Dead Sea Scrolls and Josephus) tell us a great deal about how Jews of the time of Jesus thought and lived. Some of the books, such as the Wisdom of Solomon, provide significant partial parallels, and possibly even sources, for some of the ideas in the New Testament, not least in the writings of Paul.

The 27 books of the New Testament were all written within two generations of the time of Jesus – in other words, by the end of the first century at the latest. Most scholars would put most of them earlier than that; the letters of Paul are from the late forties and the fifties, and though disputes continue as to whether he wrote all the letters that bear his name, they are the first written testimony to the explosive events of Jesus himself and the very early church.

The four canonical gospels (Matthew, Mark, Luke and John), the Acts of the Apostles, and the 13 letters ascribed to Paul were regarded by the early Christians as authentic and authoritative from very early on, by the early to middle second century at least. Doubts persisted about some books, such as Hebrews, Revelation and some of the smaller letters. Some individual churches and teachers in the second and third centuries regarded other books as authoritative, such as the 'Letter of Barnabas' and the 'Shepherd of Hermas' (both are included in what are now known as the 'Apostolic Fathers', a collection of very early Christian writings readily available in modern translations). Most early Christians, though, while valuing these writings in themselves, did not see them as on the same level as the works they saw as 'apostolic', and thus carrying a badge of authenticity.

It needs to be stressed that our evidence for the text of the New Testament is in a completely different league to our evidence for every single other book from the ancient world. We know major Greek authors like Plato and Sophocles, and even Homer, through a small handful of manuscripts, many of them medieval. We know Roman authors like Tacitus and Pliny through similarly few copies, in some cases just one or two, and many of them again very late. By contrast, we possess literally hundreds of early manuscripts of some or all of the New Testament, putting us in an unrivalled position to work back from the small variations which creep into any manuscript tradition and discern the likely original text.

Yes, scribes may have introduced alterations here and there. But the massive evidence available means that we are on extremely secure grounds for getting at what the biblical authors actually wrote.

Pressure on the church to firm up its list of authoritative books did not come, as is sometimes said today, from a desire to present a socially or politically acceptable theology; these debates were going on through periods of fierce, if intermittent, persecution. Rather, the impetus came from those who offered rival 'canons'. Some of these cut out key passages from the main books, as was done by Marcion, a Roman teacher in the second century. Others added new books with different teaching, as was done by the Gnostics, as part of their claim to possess secret teachings of what Jesus and the apostles 'really' said.

For much of church history, the churches of the East read the Bible in Greek, and the churches of the West in Latin. One of the great slogans of the sixteenth-century Reformation was that the Bible should be available to everyone in their own language, a principle which is now more or less universally acknowledged across the whole Christian world. This precipitated a flurry of translating activity in the sixteenth century itself, led not least by the German Reformer Martin Luther and the Englishman William Tyndale. Things then settled down by the seventeenth century, with the English-speaking world adopting the Authorized ('King James') Version in 1611, and remaining content with it for nearly 300 years thereafter.

As more and better new manuscripts were discovered, revealing all kinds of mostly small but interesting adjustments that needed to be made, scholars and churchmen in the late nineteenth century were persuaded that further revision was advisable. This opened the floodgates again, and the last 100 years have seen a further flurry of translations and revisions, with literally dozens now available. Similar stories can be told of translations in other languages. Organizations such as the Bible Society and the Wycliffe Bible Translators have worked tirelessly to render scripture into more and more of the world's native languages. The task is enormous, but the church has for many generations seen it as a priority.

This story, of the Bible's composition, collection and distribution, has to be told. But setting it out in this way feels a bit like trying to describe my best friend by offering a biochemical analysis of his genetic makeup. It is important. Indeed, if he didn't have that makeup he wouldn't be the same person. But there is something vital missing. It is that extra *je ne sais quoi* for which we shall now hunt.

2

Why is the Bible important?

Most Christians down the years have said something at this point about it being *inspired*. What might this mean?

People have meant a variety of different things by it. Sometimes they have really meant not inspired, but 'inspir*ing*': this book, they find, breathes new life into them. (The '-spired' bit of the word 'inspired' means, literally, 'breathed'.) But the word isn't really talking about the effect something has on us. It's talking about something that's true of the thing in itself.

At that level, people sometimes say 'the sunset was inspired', meaning (presumably) that it carried a special quality which seemed to set it apart from more mundane evenings. In the same way, people talk of a piece of music, a play, a dance, as being 'inspired'. But the sunset, and even the most sublime symphonies, are part of the general order of creation. If the point of calling the Bible 'inspired' is to say 'so it's a bit like Shakespeare, or Homer', then people may or may not agree with the assessment, but they won't be getting at what is normally meant by the word.

There are others who believe 'the inspiration of scripture' means that the Bible must be the result of an act of pure 'supernatural' intervention, bypassing the minds of the writers altogether. Those who take this view appear to envisage God either dictating books from a great distance or 'zapping' the writers with some kind of long-range linguistic thunderbolt. I suspect that many who have reacted against the idea that the Bible is actually 'inspired' in some full and rich sense are really trying to rule out that kind of statement of the idea, with all the oddities that it seems to entail. Who can blame them? After all, a glance at Paul, or Jeremiah, or Hosea is enough to indicate just how much the personality of the writer is alive and well and energetically visible within the text.

Thankfully, there is really no need for us to choose between either of those two options. Instead, I'd like you to explore with me a third option – one that views the Bible, like the sacraments, as one of the points where heaven and earth, God and humanity, overlap and interlock. Like all other such places, this is mysterious. It doesn't mean we can see at once what's going on. Indeed, it guarantees that we can't. But it does enable us to say some things which need to be said and which are otherwise difficult.

In particular, it enables us to say that the writers, compilers, editors and even collectors of scripture were people who, with different personalities, styles, methods and intentions, were none the less caught up in the strange purposes of God, purposes which included the communication, by writing, of his word. It enables us to speak about God the creator (the one we know supremely through the living Word, Jesus) being himself (so to speak) a wordsmith.

This third option enables us to see that, though words are not the only thing God specializes in, they are a central part of his repertoire. It also helps us to see that when this God is going to work within his world, he wants to work through his image-bearing human creatures, and that, since he wants to do so as far as possible with their intelligent co-operation, he wants to communicate with and through them verbally – in addition to, but also as a central point within, his many other ways of getting things said and done.

The Bible is far more, in other words, than what some people used to say a generation or so ago, that it was simply the, or a, 'record of the revelation', as though God revealed himself by some quite other means and that the Bible is simply what people wrote down to remind themselves of what had happened. The Bible offers itself, and has normally been treated in the church, as part of God's revelation, not simply a witness or echo of it. Part of the problem is the assumption that what is required is after all simply 'revelation', the communication of some kind of true information. The Bible does indeed offer plenty of information, but what it offers in a more primary way is energy for the task to which God is calling his people. Talking about the inspiration of the Bible is one way of saying that that energy comes from the work of God's Spirit.

It helps, in all this, to remind ourselves constantly what the Bible is given to us *for*. One of the most famous statements of 'inspiration' in the Bible itself puts it like this: 'all scripture is inspired by God and is useful for teaching, for reproof, for correction, and for training in righteousness, so that everyone who belongs to God may be proficient, equipped for every good work' (2 Timothy 3.16–17 NRSV). *Equipped for every good work*; there's the point. The Bible is breathed out by God (the word for 'inspired' is *theopneustos*, literally 'God-breathed') so that it can fashion and form God's people to do his work in the world.

In other words, the Bible isn't there simply to be an accurate reference point for people who want to look things up and be sure they've got them right. It is there to equip God's people to carry forward his purposes of new covenant and new creation. It is there to enable people to work for justice, to sustain their spirituality as they do so, to create and enhance relationships at every level, and to produce that new creation which will have about it something of the beauty of God himself.

* * *

One of the things Christians regularly say about the Bible is that it is 'authoritative'. But what we might mean by this has become difficult to grasp. One excellent place to begin is with something Jesus himself said about the nature of authority. Pagan rulers, he said, lord it over their subjects, but it mustn't be like that with you. Anyone who wants to be first must be the servant of all, because the Son of Man didn't come to be served, but to serve, and to give his life as a ransom for many (Mark 10.35–45). If God's authority is vested in Jesus, and if the Bible derives such authority as it has from that again, what we're talking about by calling the Bible 'authoritative' is that the Bible, somehow, becomes *an authoritative instrument*

11

of what God accomplished through Jesus, and particularly his death and resurrection.

In other words, for Jesus' death to have the effect it was intended to have, it must be communicated to the world through the 'word' of the gospel. And the Bible, in setting out the roots of the Christian story in the Old Testament and its full flowering in the New, was seen from very early on as encapsulating that powerful word, the word which communicated, and so put into effect, what God accomplished in Jesus. The Bible, in fact, is not simply an *authoritative description of* a saving plan, as though it was simply an aerial photograph of a particular piece of landscape. It is *part of the saving plan itself.* It is more like the guide who takes you round the landscape and shows you how you can enjoy it to the full.

That is why the Bible's 'authority' works in an altogether different way from the 'authority' of, say, the rules of a golf club. The Bible does indeed contain lists of rules (the Ten Commandments, for instance, in Exodus 20), but as it stands, as a whole, it does not consist of a list of dos and don'ts. It is a *story*, a grand, epic narrative that runs from the garden, where Adam and Eve look after the animals, to the city which is the Bride of the Lamb, out of which the water of life flows to refresh the world. It is, after all, a love story, albeit with a difference. And the authority of the Bible is the authority of a love story in which we are invited to take part. It is, in that sense, more like the 'authority' of a dance in which we are invited to join; or of a novel in which, though the scene is set, the plot well developed, and the ending planned and in sight, there is still some way to go, and we are invited to become living, participating, intelligent and decision-making characters within the story as it moves towards its destination.

This model of 'authority' helps us to understand how to read the Bible as Christian scripture. The 'authority' of the Old Testament is precisely the 'authority' possessed by an *earlier* scene in the novel – when we are now living in a *later* scene. It matters that the earlier scene was what it was. But it has done its job and brought us to the later scene, where some things have changed quite radically. The plot has moved forward. Even in the most postmodern of novels, characters in the final chapters do not normally repeat what they said and did near the beginning.

This doesn't mean that we are now left in a free-for-all situation where it's open to anyone to say, 'Well, we're now at a new moment in God's plan, so we can throw away anything we don't like in the old moments.' It is still the same story; and that story was, and is, the story of how the creator God is rescuing the creation from its rebellion, brokenness, corruption and death. He has accomplished this through the death and resurrection of Jesus the Messiah, in fulfilment of the promises to, and the story of, Israel.

Living with 'the authority of scripture', then, means living in the world of the story which it tells. It means soaking ourselves in it, as a community and as individuals.

Reading scripture, like praying and sharing in the sacraments, is one of the means by which the life of heaven and the life of earth interlock. (This is what older writers were referring to when they spoke of 'the means of grace'. It is not that we can control God's grace, but that there are, so to speak, places to go where God has promised to meet with his people, even if sometimes when we turn up it feels as though God has forgotten the date. More usually it is the other way round.) We read scripture in order to hear God addressing us, ourselves, here and now, today.

How this happens is unpredictable and often mysterious. *That* it happens is the testimony of millions of Christians down the years. Techniques have been developed to facilitate it, and many of them are helpful.

The way in which we 'hear' scripture, and thereby hear God's voice speaking to us through scripture, is bound up with all kinds of 'subjective' factors. None the worse for that, of course. If it isn't subjective, it isn't, in that sense, real for us. But hearing God's voice in scripture is not simply a matter of precise, technical expertise. It is a matter of love – which is the mode of knowing required for living at the intersection between heaven and earth.

Listening to God's voice in scripture does not put us in the position of having infallible opinions. It puts us where it put Jesus himself: in possession of a vocation, whether for a lifetime or for the next minute. Vocations are fragile, and are tested in performance. That is what it is like to live at the intersection of heaven and earth.

But the performance is not just about our own private pilgrimage. It is about becoming agents of God's new world – workers for justice, explorers of spirituality, makers and menders of relationships, creators of beauty. If God does indeed speak through scripture, he speaks in order to commission us for tasks like these. Christian scripture is stamped, in its shape and overall purpose and mode of use as well as its individual parts, not only with the coming together of heaven and earth, but with the overlap and interplay of present and future. It is a book designed to be read by those who are living in the present in the light of God's future, the future which has arrived in Jesus and now demands to be implemented.

3

How is the Bible to be interpreted?

There's a phrase one hears whenever the Bible is discussed both in church circles and in the wider world. 'It all depends', said a reporter on the news just a few nights ago, 'whether people are reading the Bible literally or seeing that it needs to be interpreted.' 'Some people take the Bible literally,' I recently heard a lecturer assert with great emphasis, 'while others of us see it as metaphorical.' What does it mean to 'take the Bible literally'? What would it mean to read it 'metaphorically'? Is this even a helpful way of putting the question?

Broadly speaking: No, it isn't. The old distinction between 'literal' and 'metaphorical' needs to be shaken about a bit, for a start, before we can do anything useful with it.

Ironically, considering what they mean, the words 'literal' and 'literally' have come to be used in a variety of slippery ways. Often 'literally' actually means 'metaphorically', as when a sun-bather reports, 'My arms were literally on fire after sitting there all afternoon', or an office worker says, 'The phone has literally not stopped ringing all day.' Sometimes it simply means 'really, truly', when in fact tacitly acknowledging that what is said is neither real nor true: 'My boss is literally an Adolf Hitler.'

But when it's used in relation to the Bible, it raises echoes of one controversy in particular: the interpretation of the creation story in Genesis. Nobody in America will need reminding of the polarized debates between those who insisted, and still insist, on a literal seven-day creation, and those who insisted, and still insist, on a re-reading of Genesis 1 in the light of evolutionary science. The debate that has been conducted in terms of 'creation versus evolution' has got caught up with all kinds of other debates in American culture in particular, and this has provided a singularly unhelpful backdrop to the would-be serious discussion of quite other parts of the Bible.

In fact, every Bible reader I have ever met, from whatever background or culture, has known instinctively that some parts of the Bible at least are meant literally and other parts are meant metaphorically. When the Old Testament declares that the Babylonians captured Jerusalem and burnt it down, it means, quite literally, that they captured Jerusalem and burnt it down. When Paul says that he was shipwrecked three times, he means that he was shipwrecked three times. Equally, when he says that a thief will come in the night, so that the pregnant woman will go into labour, so that you mustn't fall asleep or get drunk, but must stay awake and put on your armour (1 Thessalonians 5.1–8), it would take a particularly inept reader not to recognize one of his most spectacular mixed metaphors. And when the messenger of the Assyrian king shouts to Hezekiah's men that Egypt is a 'broken reed . . . , which will pierce the hand of anyone who leans on it' (2 Kings 18.21 NRSV), the fact that reeds grow in Egypt and that the metaphor might be quite appropriate is unlikely to blind us to the fact that it is indeed a metaphor.

Other obvious examples include the parables of Jesus. I have never yet met a reader who was under the impression that the story of the Prodigal Son had actually happened, so that if you had visited enough family farms around first-century Palestine you would eventually have run into the old father and his two sons (always supposing they made up their quarrel). Virtually all readers negotiate this point without even thinking about it. Jesus himself sometimes emphasized it (not that his hearers were likely to be mistaken on the matter) by pointing out 'literal' meanings. Sometimes the gospel writers do the same, as when Mark says that the priests realized that a particular parable was aimed against them (12.12). But this doesn't mean that the only 'truth' in the parables is the point at which they can be, so to speak, cashed out. The parables are 'true' at several quite different levels; and to recognize this is *not* a way of saying, 'So the only real "truths" that matter are things that didn't happen.' Truth (thank God) is more complicated than that, because God's world is more complicated, more interesting in fact, than that.

Another problem, a source of endless confusion, emerges at this point. In addition to the casual use of 'literally' that I mentioned a moment ago, people today use the words 'literally' and 'metaphorically' to mean two different sorts of things. On the one hand, and in accordance with the true meaning of the two words, they refer to *the way words refer to things.* 'Father' means, literally, someone who begets a child. 'A rose' refers, literally, to the flower of that name. But if I were to say to my granddaughter, 'You're my little rose', I would be denoting a person, but referring metaphorically to a flower, in order to invest the former with some at least of the attributes of the latter (pretty, fresh and sweet-smelling; not, I trust, prickly). And when a devout parishioner refers to a priest as 'Father', we assume that the reference is straightforwardly metaphorical, investing the man with paternal qualities which have nothing to do with actually begetting children. Here, the words 'literal' and 'metaphorical' are not telling us whether the things I'm talking about are abstract or concrete, but whether the words 'Father' and 'rose' are being used literally, to refer to an actual father and an actual rose, or metaphorically, to refer (not to an abstract entity, but) to actual persons who are not, in fact, fathers or roses but who we understand better by, as it were, draping those words for a moment round their necks.

But 'literal' and 'metaphorical' have come to mean, as well, something to do with *the sort of things we are referring to.* 'Was it a literal resurrection, or a metaphorical one?' We all know what the speaker is asking: did it actually happen, or not? But using 'literal' and 'metaphorical' in this way, however common it may be, is deeply confusing. It is making the word 'literal' do duty for 'concrete', and 'metaphorical' either for 'abstract' or for some other non-concrete idea ('spiritual', perhaps, though that introduces a host of further confusions).

This is only the tip of the iceberg of the discussion that we could have at this point, but there are two things I want to stress. First, we should not allow the backdrop of older, unhelpful debates about Genesis to fool us into thinking that anyone who insists that some historical part of the Bible is to be read literally, and that it intends to denote things that actually happened in concrete reality, is to be taken as some kind of a simpleton who hasn't learnt either to read texts or to live in today's real world. Nor should we allow the same polarization to make us imagine that someone who insists on reading the Bible's splendid metaphors *as* metaphors – for instance, understanding 'the Son of Man coming on the clouds' as a metaphor indicating vindication and exaltation – is a dangerous anti-literalist who has given up believing in the truth of Christianity. The Bible is full of passages which really do intend to describe things that happened in the real world – and, for that matter, to command and forbid various types of actions which occur in the real world. The God of whom the Bible speaks is, after all, the creator of that world. Part of the point of the whole story is that he loves that world and intends to rescue it, that he has put this plan into operation through a series of concrete events in actual history, and that he intends this plan to be worked out through the concrete lives and work of his people. But the Bible, like virtually all other great writing, regularly and repeatedly brings out the flavour, the meaning, the proper interpretation of these actual, concrete, space–time events by means of complex, beautiful and evocative literary forms and figures, of which metaphor is only one. Acknowledging, indeed celebrating, the intended literal reference, investigating the concrete events thus referred to, and exploring the full range of metaphorical meaning, are to be integrated together as key elements of biblical interpretation.

Second, it is then open to any reader to explore, in a particular passage, which bits are 'meant literally', which bits are 'meant metaphorically', and which bits might be both – before turning, as a second stage, to ask whether the bits which were 'meant literally' actually happened in concrete reality. This simply cannot be decided in advance by insisting either that 'everything in the Bible must be taken literally' or that we know in advance that most of it 'should be taken metaphorically'.

Take the example of the 'Son of Man' passage we referred to a moment ago, which comes from Daniel 7. The passage speaks of Daniel having a dream in which four monsters, 'beasts', come up out of the sea. Now for a start, although it is quite possible that the passage goes back to an actual person called Daniel, who had strange turbulent dreams and longed to interpret them, the book is closely related to a well-known genre that uses the conscious and deliberate construction of fictitious 'dreams' for the purpose of extended allegory. (Think of John Bunyan's *Pilgrim's Progress*.) That is a possibility we should at least hold open. Beyond that, the four 'beasts' – the lion, the leopard, the bear and the final monster with ten horns – are manifestly metaphorical. Nobody in the ancient world, or I think the modern, if asked whether Daniel's dream had come true, would investigate whether such animals 'really existed', whether you could go and see them in the wild, or in a zoo. But the fact that there were four of them was meant quite literally. It was read that way by ancient Jews (who calculated in fear and trembling where they were in the sequence). It is read that way by all modern commentators. The interesting observation that the fourth beast was almost certainly understood in the second century BC as referring to Syria, and in the first century AD as referring to Rome, merely serves to underline the fact that the metaphorical language intended a literal reference to concrete reality, even though different generations differed as to what that literal referent, that concrete reality, might be.

Again, when the dream says that the monsters 'came up out of the sea' (Daniel 7.3 NRSV), we do not regard it as a contradiction when the angel who interprets the dream says that 'four kings shall arise out of the earth' (verse 17). Many ancient Jews regarded the sea as the place and source of chaos; part of the point of Daniel 7 is that it is (ironically, in view of where this discussion began) an interpretation of Genesis 1, with life emerging from the sea and a human being eventually bringing God's order to it all. The kings come metaphorically 'from the sea'; but they are concrete kings with real-life land-based armies, not abstract entities or ideas in people's minds. And the 'coming of the Son of Man' in verse 13 is interpreted, not in the literal terms of a human figure flying around on a cloud, but in the metaphorical but thoroughly concrete terms of 'the holy ones of the Most High' (i.e. loyal Jews) 'receiving the kingdom and possessing it for ever and ever' (verse 18).

All this is a way of saying: the polarization between 'literal' and 'metaphorical' interpretation has become confused and confusing. Any who find themselves getting trapped in it should take a deep breath, read some of the Bible's glorious metaphors, think about the concrete events that the writers were referring to, and begin again.

We should take particular care to avoid one subtle but powerful line of thought. It is all too easy to suppose that, if the Bible is not really 'to be taken literally', but mostly to be interpreted 'metaphorically', that would mean that the writers, and perhaps even God, are not really interested in what we do with our own concrete circumstances, our bodily and economic and political life. Saying 'metaphorical, not literal' can lead quite quickly into the suggestion, all the more powerful for its never quite being stated head on, that God only really cares about our non-concrete, 'spiritual' life, thoughts and feelings. As soon as we find that nonsense coming up out of the sea, we should recognize it. It is the monstrous, dualistic lie which half our culture has embraced, and which the whole Bible, read literally, metaphorically, and every other way you can think of, ought to defeat and destroy. No first-century Jew would have thought like that. Nor would any early Christian, either.

The interpretation of the Bible remains, then, a huge and wonderful task. That is why we need to engage in it as far as we have time and ability. For the Bible is above all God's gift, and serious study of it can become one of the places where heaven and earth interlock, and God's future purposes arrive in the present.

4

A sample Bible study: 1 Corinthians 13

At the end of this little book you will find a short list of other publications that can help get you started in reading and interpreting the Bible – among them, my own translation of the New Testament, along with a companion series of guides to the Christian scriptures, called 'The New Testament for Everyone'.

To conclude this little book of guidance, I've chosen an edited extract from my For Everyone guide to St Paul's first letter to the Corinthians (for more information on the For Everyone guides, see the Further reading section at the back of this book). This extract is a reflection on Chapter 13, where we find Paul's beautiful, poetic 'hymn to love'. Even if you'd never read or heard any other part of the Bible, you'd probably recognize this section of Paul's letter from its frequent use in wedding ceremonies – whether in real life or in TV and film. There it's normally read aloud in the sonorous language of the classic 'King James Bible' of 1611. Here, however, I provide my own translation from the Greek text in which the poem was originally written.

¹If I speak in human languages, or even
in those of angels, but do not have love,
then I've become a clanging gong or else
a clashing cymbal. ²And if I should have
prophetic gifts, and know all mysteries,
all knowledge, too; have faith, to move the
   mountains,
but have no love – I'm nothing. ³If I give
all my possessions to the poor, and, for pride's sake,
my very body, but do not have love,
it's useless.
⁴Love's great-hearted; love is kind,
knows no jealousy, makes no fuss,
is not puffed up, ⁵no shameless ways,
doesn't force its rightful claim,
doesn't rage or bear a grudge,
⁶doesn't cheer at others' harm,
rejoices, rather, in the truth.
⁷Love bears all things, believes all things,
Love hopes all things, endures all things.

When people say, as they sometimes do, that Paul must
have been a very difficult person to have around – that
he seems to have been awkward, cantankerous, argu-
mentative, and generally an unpleasant character – this
passage is one I often quote in reply.

It seems to me impossible to imagine that this passage
could have been written in a very personal letter by the
founder of a community, to that community, *unless he
knew, and he knew that they knew, that this is the kind
of person he himself was.* Of course, that doesn't mean
that Paul lived up to this stunning picture of love
every minute of every day. But that he had (unlike

some of the teachers in Corinth) spent his life and energy being what he was and doing what he was for the sake of other people, copying and embodying the love that Jesus himself had shown in dying on the cross, I think we can be sure.

Chapter 13 doesn't stand by itself – despite the fact that, for many people, it is known mainly through being read at weddings, as though it was simply a detached poem. It is more like the slow movement of a symphony, whose first movement is chapter 12 and whose final movement is chapter 14 – the 'symphony' of Paul's teaching about the corporate worship of the church, and especially about the use of different gifts by different members of the worshipping congregation. They need to understand that they all belong together. But that won't be any good if they simply try to put the lesson into practice in a grudging or shoulder-shrugging fashion. They need to pause, to move into a different key and rhythm, and deepen their understanding of the highest virtue, the greatest quality, the most Jesus-like characteristic you can imagine: love.

The very word 'love' causes us all sorts of problems in the English language. Our vocabulary has become impoverished. Where Greek has four words, we have at most two – 'love' and 'affection'. All right, there are related ones like 'fondness' and 'compassion', but they none of them come near what Paul is talking about. The older word 'charity' has come to be associated so closely with the splendid work of organizing and administering relief for those in need that it has ceased to be useful as a translation here.

The description Paul gives in verses 4–7 is not an account of what Hollywood means by 'love'. Romantic or erotic love, at its best, is like a signpost to the thing Paul is talking about: when two people are 'in love', they often make promises which sound like verses 4–7, but the emotional and physical energy which gets them that far won't get them all the way to fulfilling the promises. It takes a commitment of mind and will – which often then, to its own surprise, brings erotic love along with it.

Nor is what Paul is talking about the same thing as we mean when we say 'I love tennis', or 'I love the colour orange'. But if we love tennis, or a colour, as much as that, we may again take the first steps of mind and will to do things which will enable us to play, or watch, more tennis, or to paint, or observe, our favourite colour.

No: what Paul has in mind is something which, though like our other loves in some ways, goes as far beyond them as sunlight goes beyond candles or electric light. Look closely for a moment at the type of person he describes in verses 4–7. This passage describes someone doing and being things which in the eyes of the world would be rubbish. The newspapers are full of the opposite every day; and most people, in ordering their own lives, assume a set of values in which what Paul is urging is at best a noble but far-off ideal.

And yet Paul insists that this 'love' is essential for Christian living, especially for communal Christian living and its shared worship. This chapter, itself the short but vital middle section of a longer whole, likewise divides into three, with the middle part being the heart of it all. The first part (verses 1–3) insists on just how vital love is; without it, nothing else matters. The middle part (verses 4–7) describes love itself, in memorable though challenging language. The final part (verses 8–13) explains that love is one of the things which will last into God's new world, and which therefore matters far, far more than the things which will pass away – which include most of the things the Corinthians were most bothered about.

Paul begins, then, by insisting that it is love that gives meaning and appropriate flavour to all other Christian living. He stacks up all the impressive things that the Corinthians might do (he says 'though *I* do these things', but the assumption is that he's talking about them), and asserts firmly that none of them are of any advantage unless there is love as well. Just as the section (chapters 12—14) and the present chapter divide into three, so also does this passage, providing a crescendo of warnings. Verse 1 declares that, without love, speaking in tongues and languages of any and every kind is simply a way of making a loud but incomprehensible noise. Verse 2 lists several of the other 'gifts' that Paul mentioned in chapter 12 and will return to in chapter 14; this time he says that without love someone who does all these things will be 'nothing' – not even a noisy gong. Verse 3 imagines someone taking one of Jesus' commands to its literal extreme, giving away all one's possessions (Mark 10.21), perhaps in order to feed the poor (the same verb can mean something like that). Paul then imagines himself handing over his body, perhaps to be tortured or to death, in order to be able, like the martyrs of old, to feel that he really had something to boast of. (Some manuscripts say 'to be burnt', which in Paul's language is a very similar word to 'boast'.) But even accomplishments like these, in the absence of love, 'won't do me any good at all'. Paul clearly imagines that on the last day those who have been justified by faith in the present will be judged according to the life they have lived (see, for instance, 3.10–15); and the one thing that will count above all else on that day is love.

But what then does he mean by 'love'? Verses 4–7, the heart of the poem at the heart of the section, describe it. Line by line of the description is clear in itself. Perhaps the best thing to do with a passage like this is to take it slowly, a line at a time, and to reflect on at least three things: first, ways in which we see this quality in Jesus himself; second, ways in which we see it (or more likely, alas, don't see it) in ourselves; and third, ways in which, if we were like that, it would work out in practice.

Such an exercise should never be undertaken simply in order to feel either good about oneself or frustrated at one's lack of moral growth. It should always be done in prayer; and at the third stage, as we ask for grace to envisage situations where we could behave differently, we should try to imagine what doing that would feel like, what steps we would have to take to make it happen, to avoid lapsing back into our normal behaviour. Then, when we're faced with the relevant situation, we will at least have a choice which we have already thought about, instead of behaving as creatures of habit. And of course the ultimate aim is for *this* way of life, peculiar though it seems and almost unbelievable at points, to become the engrained way we habitually behave. Some people have taken steps along that road ahead of us. When we meet them it's like hearing gentle music, or seeing a beautiful sunrise. But this life is within reach of each one of us; because it is the life of Jesus, the life inspired by the spirit.

Paul ends his hymn to love by inviting his readers to look ahead to God's future, in which we will discover that love of the sort he is describing will last for ever:

> [8]Love never fails. But prophecies will be
> abolished; tongues will stop, and knowledge, too,
> be done away. [9]We know, you see, in part;
> we prophesy in part; [10]but, with perfection,
> the partial is abolished. [11]As a child
> I spoke, and thought, and reasoned like a child;
> when I grew up, I threw off childish ways.
> [12]For at the moment all that we can see
> are puzzling reflections in a mirror;
> then, face to face. I know in part, for now;
> but then I'll know completely, through and through,
> even as I'm completely known. So, now,
> faith, hope, and love remain, these three; and, of
>   them all,
> love is the greatest.

When Wolfgang Amadeus Mozart was a young man, living with his father Leopold (himself a fine musician) in Vienna, he is said to have played a trick on him from time to time. Young Wolfgang would come home from spending a riotous evening with his friends; his father would already be asleep in bed. Wolfgang would go to the piano, and would play, loudly, a rising scale of notes, getting slower and louder as they reached the resolution at the top of the scale . . . and then he would stop, one note short, and go to bed himself.

Old Leopold, so the story goes, would toss and turn in bed as the unfinished scale came into his dreams and imagination. The frustration of having one's musical senses aroused in that way without resolution would become too hard to bear. Eventually he would have to drag himself from his slumbers, stagger downstairs, and play the last note.

No doubt he had ways of getting his own back, but that is another story. What we are concerned with here is the way in which Paul describes the call of love, and of life itself, as an unfinished scale, going ahead of us into God's future. The music of love, which will one day be completed, is therefore not just our duty. It is our destiny.

Consider that distinction for a moment. So often the moral demands of the Christian life are presented within a framework which speaks of duty: a cold, hard slog to attain a distant and seemingly impossible standard. But Paul sees all of life within the framework of God's future – God's future which has burst into the present in the person of Jesus of Nazareth, and especially in his resurrection, which has marked him out as God's Messiah, the world's true Lord. In that future, Paul sees a world of joy, delight, and above all of love. So in the present there are three things which point into the future (verse 13): faith, which looks at the God made known in Jesus and trusts him for everything; hope, which looks ahead to God and what he will do in the future, which is already assured by Jesus' resurrection; and love, which will finally know as it is known, and embrace as it is already embraced (see 8.3, and e.g. Galatians 2.19–20 and 4.9).

Paul places these abiding certainties over against the things which the Corinthians were priding themselves on. Prophecy? Who will need it in the world to come? Tongues? Why would we need to speak them in the world where everyone understands everyone else at once? Special knowledge? We shall all know everything we can know and need to know. These are things which belong to the country we live in at the moment. Love is God's river, flowing on into the future, across the border into the country where there is no pride, no jostling for position, no contention among God's people. We are invited to step into that river here and now, and let it take us where it's going.

Paul wants the Corinthians, above all, to learn to think in terms of God's future and its relation to the present. So here, as he draws this poetic little chapter to its close, he uses three images that speak of the transition from the present to the future, the transition which makes it all the more important to make love the centre of their lives here and now.

The first image is of the child growing to maturity. 'When I grew up, I stopped behaving like a child.' Tongues, prophecy, clever-sounding words of knowledge: child's play, says Paul. Give me the grown-up stuff, the real spiritual, emotional and personal maturity. Give me the humanness that will last, enhanced and unimpeded, through to God's new world. Give me, in other words, love: the love described here, the love which is the highest form of knowing and being humans can attain in this world or the world to come.

The second image is of the mirror. Mirrors were made in Corinth, but the point Paul is making is familiar to many writers in the ancient world. When you look in the mirror everything is back to front, inside out. You can't always make out what it is you're looking at. That's what the present time is like, Paul is saying. You can see something of God's plan, something of what's going on, something of what God wants for his human creatures. But in the world to come all will be plain. 'Face to face' could be simply a way of saying 'so we won't be looking in mirrors any longer', but it is probably also a way of reminding his readers, as John puts it in his first letter, that when Jesus appears we shall be like him, 'because we shall see him as he is' (1 John 3.2).

This leads to the third way of saying the same thing, which picks up the contrast in verses 9 and 10 between things that are partial and things that are complete. 'Now I know in part'; there is such a thing as genuine Christian knowledge in the present, even though 'knowledge' can 'puff you up' (8.1). But then – in God's new world, the world waiting to be born, the world already glimpsed in Jesus' resurrection – 'then I shall know in the same way that I too have been known.' What matters at the moment is not your knowledge of God, but God's knowledge of you; but your knowledge, too, will be complete in the age to come.

Think within God's time-plan, Paul is urging them. If you do that, you will not only see how important love is. You will be able to resist the temptation to factional fighting, to perpetuating social divisions at the Lord's supper, and to boasting over spiritual gifts (all of which are problems he addresses elsewhere in this letter). Love, at present an unfinished scale, is what will last into God's new world. And one day the Son himself will come down and complete the music.

Further reading

Here is a short list of books that can guide you further in your exploration of the topics discussed in this book. All are available through bookshops, or direct from the publisher at <www.spckpublishing.co.uk>.

The first three chapters of *Why Read the Bible?* are drawn from chapters 13 and 14 of the author's *Simply Christian* (London, SPCK; San Francisco, HarperOne, 2006), and Chapter 4 is based on pages 171–9 of his *Paul for Everyone: 1 Corinthians* (London, SPCK; Louisville, KY, Westminster John Knox, 2003).

For more information on *Simply Christian* visit: <www. spckpublishing.co.uk/shop/simply-christian-reissue/>.

For more information on *Paul for Everyone: 1 Corinthians* visit: <www.spckpublishing.co.uk/shop/paul-for-everyone-1-corinthians/>.

The For Everyone Commentary Library is published as a limited-edition boxed set, which can be viewed at: <www. spckpublishing.co.uk/shop/tom-wrights-for-everyone-commentary-library/>.

The set comprises 18 volumes, which may also be obtained separately.

The complete *New Testament for Everyone* translation is also available in stand-alone hardback edition: <www.spckpublishing. co.uk/shop/the-new-testament-for-everyone/>.

Other books by the same author (all published by SPCK):

Finding God in the Psalms: Sing, Pray, Live (2014)
How God Became King: Getting to the heart of the Gospels (2012)

Further reading

The Lord and His Prayer (SPCK Classics, 2012)
New Testament Prayer for Everyone (2012)
New Testament Wisdom for Everyone (2013)
Scripture and the Authority of God: How to read the Bible today (second edition, 2013)
Simply Good News: Why the gospel is news, and what makes it good (2015)
Simply Jesus: Who he was, what he did, why it matters (2011)
Surprised by Scripture: Engaging with contemporary issues (2014)